A
Sketchbook of the
Union Infantryman

Written and Illustrated by
Alan H. Archambault

 Thomas Publications
Gettysburg, PA 17325

Contents

Introduction
A Patriot Heritage
The Militia
The Regular Army
The Call to Arms
Enlisting
The Union Volunteer
Hayfoot, Strawfoot
Off to the Front
The Union Infantryman
The Regiment in Battle
Seeing the Elephant
Trial By Fire
Forage Caps
Hats
Basic Uniform
The Frock Coat
The Sack Coat
Overcoats
Footwear
Pistols and Knives
Canteens
Haversacks
Knapsacks and Blanket Rolls
Cartridge Boxes and Cap Pouches
Accouterments
Smoothbore Muskets
Bayonets
Rifles
U.S. Rifle Muskets
Loading a Rifle Musket
British Weapons for Yankees
Firearms from the Continent
Union Sharpshooters
Arms of the Sharpshooters

Repeating Firearms
Heroism
The National Colors
The Regimental Colors
Infantry Officers
Symbols of Command
Noncommissioned Officers
NCO Rank and insignia
Patriots from Many Lands
Sons of Erin
Zouaves
Corps Badges
Discipline
Rations
Recreation
A "Civil" War
Tenting Tonight
Winter Quarters
Taking Cover
Digging In
Health and Hygiene
The Veteran Reserve Corps
Black Infantrymen
Women of the Infantry
Pets and Mascots
Brave Drummer Boys
Captured
Wounded
A Soldier's Death
A Soldier's Resting Place
A Compassionate Victor
The Grand Review
Mustering Out
Union Veterans
The Legacy

Introduction

This sketchbook has been created to serve as an introduction to the life and times of the Federal infantryman during his war to preserve the Union during the period 1861 to 1865. As a sketchbook, the emphasis is on the visual elements of the infantryman's world, but it also gives insight into his motivations and inspirations that sustained him through four years of terrible conflict.

When the conflict began in 1861, the men, boys, and women who answered the call to preserve the Federal Union did so with as much dedication and enthusiasm as those sons and daughters of the South who saw their states' rights being threatened. Once the war proved to be a deadly contest, and the early enthusiasm waned, the Confederates' motivation for service and sacrifice was linked to the concrete task of driving the Northern invaders from their soil. The Union soldiers had to settle for their beliefs in the importance of maintaining a strong union of states and, for some, the abolition of slavery. In spite of the North's superiority in human and material resources, the outcome of the war was in doubt right up to the very end of the struggle.

This sketchbook strives to evoke a little bit of the spirit of the Union infantryman by presenting aspects of the conflict from his perspective. It is hoped that readers of this work, particularly young people, gain some understanding and appreciation for the service and sacrifices of the "Boys in Blue." Their legacy is an intregal part of our shared American heritage.

A Patriot Heritage. Although the Patriots of the American Revolution had passed on into history prior to the crisis of 1861, their legacy of sacrifice and valor was an inspiration for the Northern soldier. As children, many of the men who later served in the Union Army listened to the stirring stories told by the local veterans of the Revolution and the War of 1812. In the days before sports celebrities and movie stars, veterans and frontier heroes were the idols of the nation's citizens. Letters, speeches and editorials of the period indicate that many Union soldiers were very mindful of the responsibility to preserve the union of states created by the blood and bravery of their Revolutionary ancestors on the battlefields of Lexington, Saratoga and Yorktown.

The Militia. Since colonial days, the male citizens of the various states were expected to be enrolled in the militia, subject to be called on to defend their communities. Although in times of peace the militia laws were seldom enforced, many Northern communities boasted volunteer military companies. These units were usually chartered to defend the local area from enemies both "foreign and domestic." Most of these units wore colorful uniforms and had long, celebrated histories. Some units chose uniforms reflecting their Revolutionary War heritage, while others copied popular European military fashions. The units were both social and military in nature and their members were often the most respected members of the community. When the Union was threatened in 1861, the various militia companies were summoned from the Northern states and served as the nucleus around which the state volunteer regiments were formed. A few of the many militia units of the North are illustrated here. They are, from left to right: Private of the Putnam Phalanx of Connecticut; Company Officer, 71st Regiment (the American Guard); New York State Militia; Private, Cincinnati Rover Guards, Ohio Militia; Sergeant, Albany Burgesses Corps, New York State Militia.

The Regular Infantry on the Eve of War. Beginning during the War of Independence against Britain, the American infantry had been the muscle of the United States Army. The foot soldier had won our independence, defended our nation's honor in the War of 1812, protected the frontier, and fought Mexico in a war for "Manifest Destiny." In 1860, as the nation faced an internal conflict, the Regular Army numbered only 1,108 officers and 15,259 men. Taking into account those soldiers who were sick, absent from duty, or confined, the Army consisted of about 14,000 effective soldiers. The units were dispersed all over the continent, with most serving on the western frontier. While serving at remote garrisons, many of the soldiers took an interest in the events that would split the nation. When the storm broke in April 1861, the ten existing infantry regiments of the United States Army would become the nucleus for the Union infantry. This illustration depicts a first sergeant, a private and a musician of Company B, 4th U.S. Infantry Regiment in full dress uniforms. The 4th Infantry served on the Pacific Coast from 1853 until recalled east in 1861. The regiment went on to serve with the Union Army of the Potomac and fought, with honor, in twelve major campaigns.

The Call to Arms. On April 12, 1861, Confederate forces fired on the Federal garrison at Fort Sumter, South Carolina. This act of war sent the North into a flurry of "war fever." On April 15, President Abraham Lincoln called for volunteers to crush the rebellion against the Federal Union. Soon, patriotic rallies were held throughout the North and young men were eager to punish the "traitors" for their insult to the flag of the United States. The ranks of the volunteer companies were soon filled with eager recruits, ready to prove their loyalty and courage. Indeed, one of the biggest fears of the eager volunteers was that the war would be over before they could prove themselves in battle against the Rebels.

Enlisting. Fueled by the patriotism generated by the war rally or recruiting officer, the new volunteers were ready to "answer the call." First they would fill out enlistment forms, undergo a routine, and often inadequate, medical examination, and finally take an oath, swearing to defend the Union and obey their officers. When volunteers were under the age of eighteen they needed their parents' permission to enlist, usually as a drummer boy. However, some eager underage recruits would write the number eighteen on a piece of paper and slip it in their shoe prior to enlisting. In this manner they could honestly claim to be "over eighteen," without lying to their government.

The Union Volunteer. Once mustered into the service of his "Uncle Sam," the Union volunteer aspired to become a soldier in the best tradition of the service. In many cases the soldiers of the regular Army, or as the war progressed, the battle tested veteran units, served as role models for the young recruits. Throughout the war, there were always numbers of young men reaching military age who were eager and willing to serve regardless of the perils of war. The average Union soldier was white, Protestant, native-born, unmarried, and between 18 and 29 years of age with the largest single group being those of age 18. Statistics indicate that most Yankee volunteers stood between 5 feet, 5 inches and 5 feet 9 inches in height and weighed 143 pounds. About half of the Union recruits came from the farms of the North, but many other trades and occupations were also represented.

"Hayfoot, Strawfoot." Although the new recruits were eager, few had any military experience or training. Many of the young recruits had never been very far from home before and homesickness was a major problem in the Army camps. It is claimed that some of the raw recruits were so lacking in basic education that they did not know their left foot from their right. Since about forty-eight percent of the Yankee recruits were farmboys, the drill sergeants would sometimes tie pieces of hay to one foot and straw to the other. Although the rural recruits may not have known their right from left, they certainly knew the difference between hay and straw. Therefore, the sergeants would march them to the command of "hayfoot, strawfoot!" Soon, many new recruits were nicknamed "strawfoots."

Off to the Front. After a period of organization and training (usually far too short), the companies of volunteer infantry were formed into regiments. Soon after, orders usually came for the unit to muster at a designated place and leave for the war. Many troops were transported by train, while others took ships. The day of departure was full of emotion, pride and sadness. It was a scene that was enacted in towns, villages and cities throughout the North. Many young soldiers were leaving home for the first time, while married men were leaving their wives and children. All were determined to defend the Union. For many men it would be the last time they would see their loved ones. Little did the volunteers, particularly in the early days of the war, realize the dangers and hardships which lay ahead in their struggle to preserve the Union. It would be a long, heartbreaking road to "see the dawn of peace."

The Union Infantryman. The backbone of the Federal Army during the war to preserve the Union was the infantryman. It was he who shouldered the musket and went forth into battle to decide the survival of the Union. Perhaps one of the strongest virtues of the Yankee foot soldier was his willingness to stand by his government through difficult times. During the course of the war, the Northern forces suffered many disappointing setbacks, particularly in the early campaigns. Although the Union infantryman was often defeated and sometimes disheartened, he was always willing to "rally 'round the flag" once again and have another try at defeating the seemingly invincible Confederates. Eventually, the perseverance and dedication of the "Boys in Blue" led to ultimate victory over their brave Southern foes.

The Union Regiment in Battle. The infantry regiments of the Union usually fought in a linear battle formation, two ranks deep. A line of skirmishers was often deployed in advance of the main battle line to "feel" out the enemy. The regimental and national colors were carried in the center of the line while smaller unit flags were sometimes carried on the regiment's flanks to mark their position. A full regiment of infantry consisted of ten companies of 100 men each, totaling 1000 enlisted men. A regiment was commanded by a colonel and each company by a captain. Other staff officers brought the total officers assigned to a regiment to 37. Few regiments actually took the field at full strength since illness and death took its toll. As the war progressed some regiments were whittled down to only several hundred men.

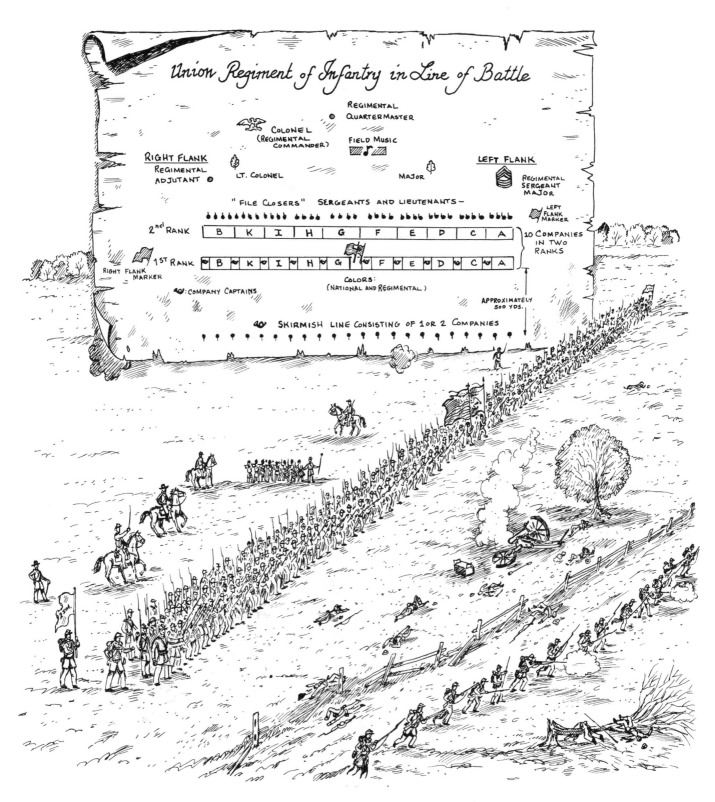

"Seeing the Elephant." Very few of the young soldiers in the Union infantry had ever been engaged in armed conflict prior to their enlistment in the Army. In fact, many young men had never even journeyed very far from their hometowns. Therefore, the prospect of traveling far from home and engaging in a historic battle was considered a rare and unique event. For most Americans of the 1860s this experience could be compared to seeing an elephant: a curious creature that they knew existed, but one few Americans had the chance to see. During the war "seeing the elephant" became soldier slang for engaging in battle. A soldier who had seen the elephant was considered a combat veteran.

Trial By Fire. The true test of the infantryman's courage, dedication, and discipline was to be found on the battlefield. The brutal nature of combat and death came as a rude shock to many Union infantrymen, who had only viewed idealized depictions of combat in prints and books. Many young infantrymen believed that battles would be exciting, organized and decisive. They believed that bravery would be rewarded and that death, if it came, would be painless and noble. Of course, the reality was that combat was usually chaotic and always full of fear, death, and suffering. However unprepared the average Union infantryman was for the realities of combat, most soldiers performed with amazing courage. Observers have stated that the American soldier fought with less fanfare, and more raw courage and resolution, than the soldiers of Europe. Although less celebrated than his Confederate foe, the Union infantryman often fought with legendary valor. The stress of combat and campaigning took its toll on many of the Union's best infantry regiments, and by mid-war many units were down from a thousand men to several hundred. However, this did not stop them from fighting with skill and courage that is remembered to this day. This illustration depicts the defense of Little Round Top at Gettysburg by the outnumbered infantrymen of the 20th Maine Regiment on the afternoon of July 2, 1863. After a grueling march, the men were rushed to the defense of the hill just before the Confederates attacked. The men held their critical position and maintained a withering fire on the gray attackers until they ran out of ammunition. Faced with continued attacks, and many casualties, the Maine men were ordered to fix bayonets. Led by their innovative commander, Colonel Joshua Chamberlain, their unexpected bayonet charge swept the Rebel attackers from the hill and helped save the left flank of the Union position.

Forage Caps. The most distinctive uniform item of the Civil War was the forage cap. There were actually several different styles of forage cap worn by Union infantrymen during the war. **1.** Cap worn with the visor flipped up to give the soldier a jaunty look. **2.** Union infantry officer wearing a French inspired "Chasseur" style forage cap with an embroided infantry hunting horn insignia. **3.** New York Militiaman wearing a gray "Chasseur" style forage cap. **4.** Black infantryman wearing a Model 1858 forage cap. This style was often called a "bummer's cap." His cap is adorned with a brass infantry hunting horn with a regimental number in the center and the company letter above. **5.** Forage cap covered by a white linen "havelock." The havelock was designed to keep the sun off the head and neck of the soldier in warm weather. Most soldiers found them impractical and soon used them as handkerchiefs or dishrags. **6.** Union infantryman wearing the Model 1858 forage cap. Period photographs indicate that the cap was often worn without any type of insignia. **7.** Army regulations authorized a company letter to be worn on the cap. **8.** In rainy weather, a waterproof oilcloth cover was often worn over the forage cap. **9.** The chinstrap of the cap could be worn down to keep the cap in place. **10.** The "McDowell" style cap featured a sloping visor and large crown. It was named after the Federal general. This infantryman wears a cloth Third Corps badge on the cap.

Hats. Many Union infantrymen preferred the comfort of a slouch hat over that of a cap. Illustrated here are a few of the many styles worn during the war. **1.** Officer in private purchase hat with infantry insignia and hat cords. **2.** Young infantryman wearing civilian style hat with Third Corps insignia. **3.** Black infantryman in another common style of civilian hat. **4.** Infantryman wearing the Model 1858 hat without insignia. **5.** Infantryman in full dress uniform wearing the regulation Model 1858 "Jeff Davis" hat with infantry insignia, unit designation, ostrich plume, and light blue hat cord. **6.** Soldier in straw hat. **7.** Infantryman wearing a wide brimmed slouch hat. This style was very popular in the western armies. **8.** Another style of slouch hat popular in both Eastern and Western Theaters.

The Infantryman's Basic Uniform. To the eager volunteers of 1861, one of the inducements of military service was the appeal of blue uniforms and brass buttons. This illustration depicts the basic dress of the Union infantryman as he would have appeared early in the conflict. His undershirt is made of white wool flannel, which many soldiers found uncomfortable and replaced with civilian style shirts sent from home. His wool flannel "long johns" are equipped with drawstrings to keep them from riding up his leg and to prevent "critters" from crawling up. His frock coat is made of dark blue wool broadcloth with standing collar. It was adorned with nine eagle buttons down the front and two small buttons at each cuff. The collar and cuffs are piped with light blue, to indicate the infantry branch. In the early months of the war, Union soldiers were authorized to wear dark blue trousers, but in December 1861, they were replaced with less expensive trousers made of sky blue kersey cloth. Since belt loops did not come into wide usage until the early 1900s, his trousers are held up with suspenders.

The Frock Coat. In the first years of the war, many Union infantryman served in the field clad in the attractive uniform coat, popularly known as a frock coat. On full dress occasions this garment could be fitted with brass shoulder scales, but on campaign it was generally worn unadorned. This infantryman also wears a Model 1858 forage cap and sky blue wool trousers. His waistbelt holds his cap pouch and bayonet scabbard and his cartridge box is slung on his right hip. His canteen and haversack rest on his left side. He is armed with an imported British Enfield rifle musket and bayonet. As the war progressed, the simpler, less expensive, sack coat saw increased use, but many soldiers continued to wear the frock coat throughout the conflict.

Alan H. Archambault

20

The Sack Coat. One of the most common items of uniform worn by the Union infantryman was the sack coat, or fatigue blouse. Although it was adopted by the Army prior to the war, it came into widest use as a result of wartime requirements. Originally, it was designed to be worn only while on fatigue details, while the more "military" frock coat would be worn on campaign and in battle. With the vast number of volunteers brought into the Union Army at the beginning of the war, it was soon found that the sack coat made an economical alternative to the frock coat. The utilitarian fatigue blouse saw extensive use in every theater of the war. Eventually, over a dozen private government contractors, as well as Federal clothing depots were producing sack coats. There were several variations in design but they were all made of dark blue wool flannel with a turn-over collar and four brass uniform buttons. The coat was worn loose and was issued in only four sizes. Clad in his simple sack coat, the Union infantryman was probably the most humbly dressed, yet most effective fighting man in the world, equaled only by his Confederate foe.

Alan W. Archambault

21

Overcoats. During the colder months Union infantrymen were issued overcoats to protect them from the elements. The standard Federal pattern worn by most infantrymen was made of sky blue wool kersey. It was single breasted with a standing collar and a cape which reached to the soldier's elbow. It also had large cuffs which could be folded down over the soldier's hands for warmth. Generally, the overcoats were put in storage in the spring and returned to the soldiers in the autumn. When the weather turned unseasonably warm it was not unusual for inexperienced soldiers to throw away their overcoats to lighten their burdens during a march. However, they soon regretted their actions when the weather turned cold again. One interesting story regarding overcoats took place during the Battle of Stones River, Tennessee. On December 31, 1862, retreating Union soldiers left a row of overcoats on the battlefield. The attacking Confederates mistook them for live Yankees and riddled them with musket fire.

In Stormy Weather the Cape could be thrown up over the head.

Standing Collar was often turned down for Comfort.

Infantryman's Overcoat with Cape.

Back View with Cape removed to Show Construction details.

22

Footwear. Napoleon is said to have remarked that, "an army moves on its stomach," but it may be stated, more literally, that an infantryman moves on his feet. Therefore, good footwear is one of the most important requirements for a foot soldier. The most common style of footwear issued to Union infantrymen was the Jefferson Boot, or as it was often called, the bootee. They were made of cowhide, ankle high and secured with a leather lace. Although not very attractive, and often called "gunboats" by the soldiers, the booties were rugged, generally comfortable and saw extensive service throughout the war. When on campaign, some soldiers pulled their socks up over their trouser legs in order to keep insects and dirt out. Some units also adopted leather or canvas gaiters to protect their lower legs and boots. However, these gaiters proved to be unpopular and were generally discarded. Some men preferred to wear more traditional boots and many types were privately purchased by both officers and men. These ranged from low "half" boots to "Wellington" style calf high boots. Government issue socks were generally made of gray wool but many socks of various colors and fabrics were also purchased or sent from home.

Pistols and Knives. In the early days of the war, few self-respecting volunteer infantrymen would consider themselves fully armed without a revolver and "Bowie" knife. Although the government did not issue these weapons to the men, believing that a musket or rifle was sufficient, the troops thought they knew better. Before leaving for the war, many infantrymen were given knives or revolvers as gifts from relatives, friends, or local communities. Often the knives featured patriotic inscriptions while the revolvers ranged from large "horse pistols" to the popular "pocket" models made by Colt and other manufacturers. However, once on the battlefield, the men generally found that they never got close enough to the enemy to use these weapons. In addition, the pistols and knives were clumsy to carry on long marches. As a result, most of these personal weapons were either discarded or sent home after the first campaign. Most infantrymen learned that their best defense on the battlefield was discipline and a government-issued rifle or musket. The illustration depicts an infantryman of the First Rhode Island Detached Militia demonstrating his pistol to a member of the First Fire Zouaves, 11th New York Volunteers, who wields a fighting knife.

Canteens. One of the most valued items of equipage issued to Union infantrymen was the canteen. The illustration depicts several of the many patterns available to Union soldiers. **a.** Gutta Percha canteen. This prewar style was made with a cloth fabric exterior and vulcanized gutta-percha (similar to India-rubber) interior. **b.** U.S. Model 1858 canteen. This style became the most widely used of the war. It was made of two pieces of tinned metal soldered together and covered with gray, blue, or brown wool. Early war canteens featured a leather strap which was replaced, in 1862, with a white cotton sling. The spout was made of pewter closed with a cork stopper secured to the canteen with a cord or chain. **c.** Side view of Model 1858 canteen. **d.** Improved Model 1858 "Bullseye" canteen with concentric rings pressed into the sides of the canteen for added strength (shown with cover removed). **e.** Canteen with water filter patented by Charles Bartholomae in 1861 (top view shows kidney shape). **f.** Cantel Patent Leather canteen with tinfoil interior and joined with copper rivets. **g.** Drinking cups made of tinned iron.

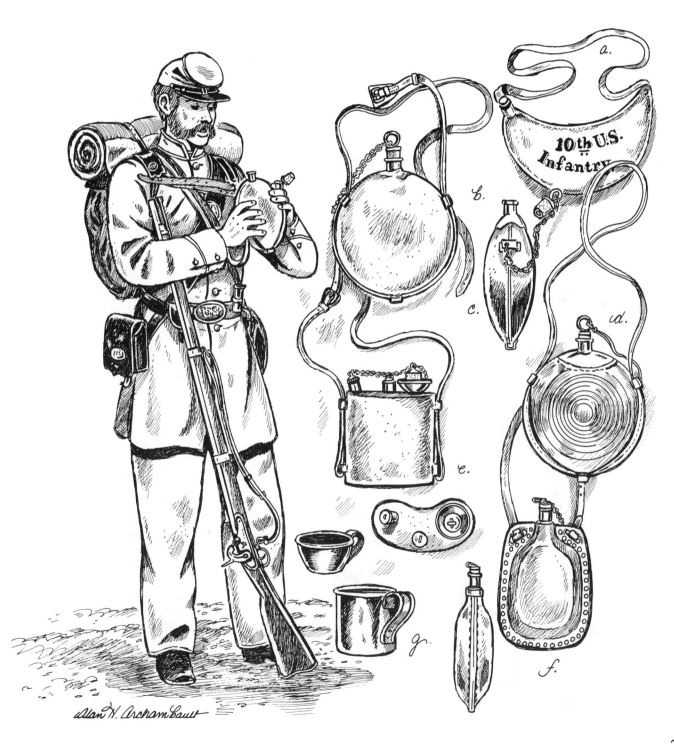

25

Haversacks. The Union infantryman carried his rations of food and small personal belongings in a haversack. The haversack was usually carried over the right shoulder, and rested on the left hip. The regulation Federal issue haversack was made of canvas which was waterproofed with black paint. Buttoned into the interior of the haversack was a removeable bag of unpainted canvas. A number of states issued haversacks of various patterns. Most of these were made of white canvas or linen. This illustration depicts some of the many items carried by the Union infantryman in his haversack. From the left are: a sewing kit, called a "housewife." Pen, ink and stationary. Candle and holder. Tobacco, pipe and matches. Camp mirror, comb, shaving soap and brush, razor and its case. Mess plate and utensils. Potatoes, onion and carrot. Toothbrush. Bible and dictionary. Photograph of loved one. Diary and pencil. Ration of salt pork. Coffee cup. Coffee beans and bag of sugar. Hardtack crackers.

Knapsacks and Blanket Rolls. At the beginning of their service, most Union infantrymen were issued knapsacks designed to carry their blankets, shelter half and extra clothing. These packs were designed to be worn squarely on the back and were supported by leather straps worn over the shoulders and across the chest. Many soldiers found these packs uncomfortable on campaign and discarded them at their first opportunity. Often extra clothing would be rolled in a wool blanket and perhaps a waterproof "gum" blanket, tied with a piece of rope or leather strap, and slung over the shoulder. However, many veterans came to appreciate the convenience and protection of the Army issue knapsack, and continued to use them throughout the war.

A number of different styles of knapsacks were worn by Union infantrymen during the course of the war. Early in the conflict, many states issued rigid-frame knapsacks made of leather or painted canvas supported by wood frames. Although these packs looked good on parade they were heavy, awkward, and ultimately impractical for campaigning. The most widely issued knapsacks were nonrigid types made of rubberized cloth or painted canvas. The U.S. Army regulation model was adopted in 1858 and consisted of two compartments to hold the soldier's extra clothing, blankets, or shelter half. The knapsack was made of black rubberized canvas with russet leather straps. Often unit designations were painted or stenciled on the pack. The knapsack was usually topped by a blanket or overcoat which was rolled up and secured to the pack with leather straps. A waterproof "gum" blanket could also be placed over the blanket to protect it from the elements in wet weather. This illustration depicts: **a.** Back view of M 1858 knapsack showing the attachment of a wool blanket wrapped in a "gum" blanket. **b.** Front view showing the arrangement of straps. **c.** Open view showing compartments. **d.** Back and side view of a rigid knapsack. **e.** Waterproof "gum" blanket. **f.** Blanket roll containing spare clothing, and worn over the soldier's shoulder. **g.** Blanket rolled up and carried on the back suspended by a strap.

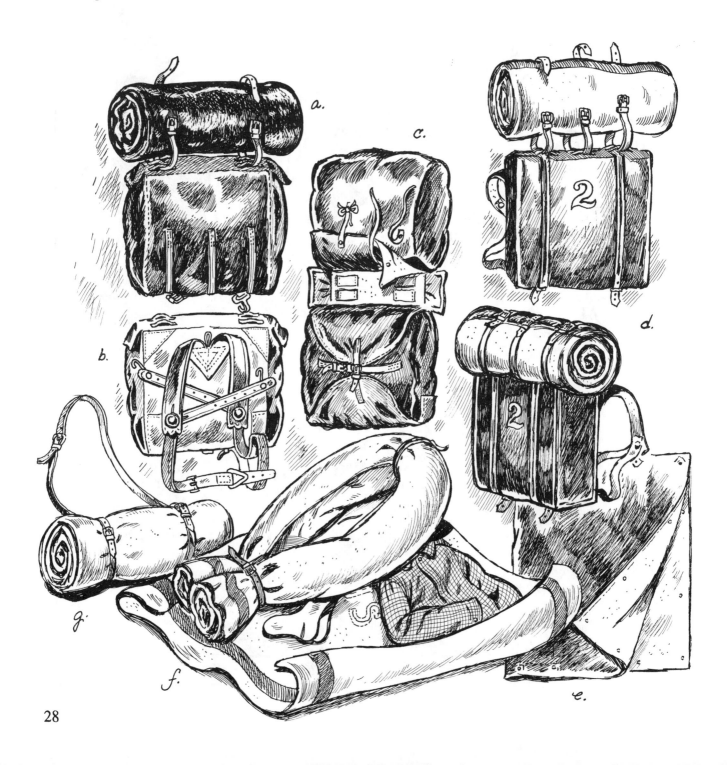

Cartridge Boxes and Cap Pouches. In order for the average Union infantryman to be effective on the battlefield, he needed to have dry, intact cartridges and percussion caps readily available. Therefore, among his most important accouterments was his leather cartridge box and cap pouch. The cartridge box was designed to be worn on either a shoulder sling or on a waistbelt. It was made of stout leather, dyed black, with a large flap which protected the vulnerable cartridges from the elements. Two tinned metal containers fit into the box. These "tins" held the cartridges in place. The typical infantry cartridge box held forty rounds of ammunition. The cartridges were made up of a bullet and a pre-measured powder charge wrapped in paper. The cartridges were issued in packages of ten along with twelve percussion caps. The soldier would fill the top section of the cartridge box tins with loose cartridges and place unopened packages in the compartments below, until he was ready to use them. Usually, a brass "U.S." plate was fitted on the flap on the box, while a circular "eagle" breastplate was worn on the sling. The cap pouch was worn on the waistbelt near the belt plate. A piece of fleece kept the small copper percussion caps from falling out when the pouch was open. A small wire pick was also carried in the pouch to open a clogged rifle cone.

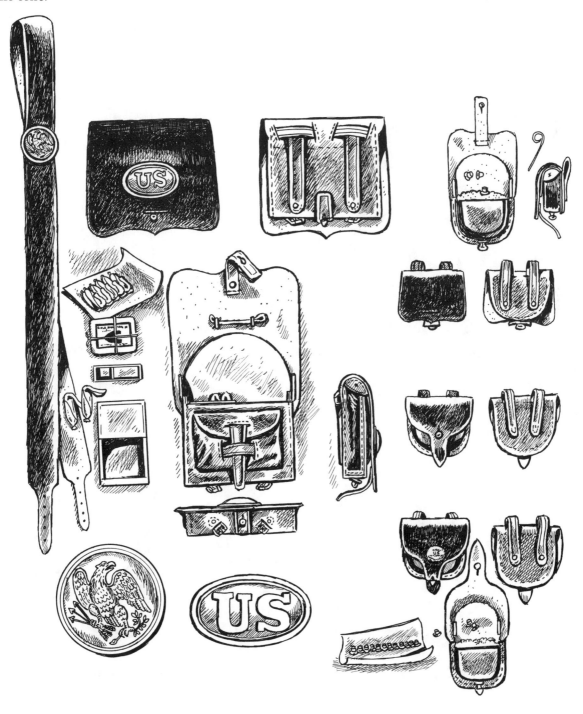

Accouterments. On the battlefield, Union soldiers wore their accouterments in a manner that would allow them easy access to their ammunition. Often, extra baggage, like knapsacks or overcoats, were taken off and placed in a safe area. However, haversacks, canteens, cartridge boxes and cap pouches were all worn into battle. When on the firing line, cartridge boxes and cap pouches were often swung around to the front of the soldier and the flap of the cartridge box turned back behind the waistbelt. This aided the soldier in quickly loading his weapon.

© Alan H. Archambault

Smoothbore Muskets. In the early days of the war, many Union infantrymen were armed with a number of obsolete smoothbore muskets. Most of these weapons were made at the Springfield or Harpers Ferry Arsenals, and many were veterans of earlier conflicts. The muskets were .69 caliber and could fire a single round ball or a combination of a .69 caliber ball and three smaller balls, called "buck and ball." These smoothbore weapons had an effective range of 50 to 100 yards. A few of the early flintlock models saw limited service during the early stage of the conflict, but most of the flintlocks had been converted to the percussion ignition system in the 1850s and thousands of these were issued to Union infantrymen. The U.S. Musket, Model 1842, was the first American musket produced in the percussion cap system and many regiments of Federal foot soldiers were armed with this model. However, as the range and accuracy of the rifle muskets became evident, most infantrymen exchanged their smoothbores for the newer rifled arms as they became available.

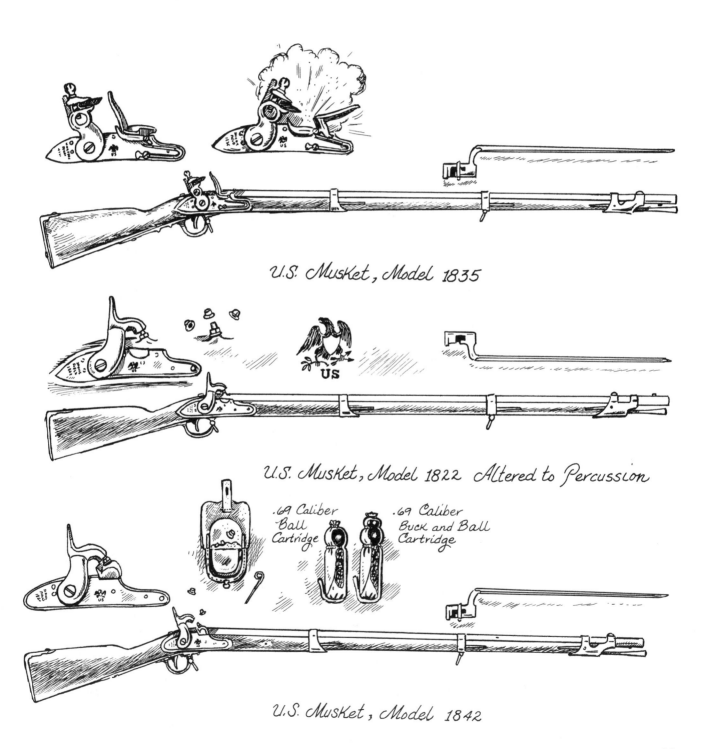

U.S. Musket, Model 1835

U.S. Musket, Model 1822 Altered to Percussion

.69 Caliber Ball Cartridge   .69 Caliber Buck and Ball Cartridge

U.S. Musket, Model 1842

Bayonets. In the days of the smoothbore musket, battles were often decided on the points of the bayonet. However, by the 1860s the rifle musket was destined to rule the battlefield. The increased accuracy of the rifle musket, as well as the fire power of breechloaders and repeating firearms, meant that battle lines seldom reached the point where bayonets and swords were of much importance. Most soldiers and their officers preferred to use fire power to decide the engagement. As a result, bayonets still looked deadly, but few soldiers actually fell victim to them. This did not mean that bayonets were not important to the soldiers. They were often employed as candle holders, can openers, and cooking spits. Soldiers could also use a musket and bayonet to support their tents and to help construct a rifle pit. Bayonets came in two basic styles. The socket bayonet had a thin triangular blade and was secured to the musket by a socket and retaining ring. Most socket bayonets had 18 inch blades and were the most common style of the war. The saber bayonet was manufactured to fit on several types of rifles. It featured a long, unwieldy, sword blade which looked fearsome but was rather impractical to carry and use on the battlefield.

Rifles. In 1841, prior to the War for the Union, the U.S. Army adopted a percussion rifle for the use of elite troops. This weapon became known as the "Mississippi Rifle" after its use in the Mexican War by members of Jefferson Davis' volunteer unit from that state. Originally, the Model 1841 was produced in .54 caliber, but beginning in 1855, many were rerifled to .58 caliber and fitted with a bayonet lug and long range sights. The Model 1855 rifle was produced at the Harpers Ferry Armory from 1857 to 1861. It was produced in .58 caliber and was fitted with the same saber bayonet as the altered Mississippi Rifle. Both rifles were valued for their beauty and accuracy and were extensively used by Federal infantrymen in their efforts to preserve the Union.

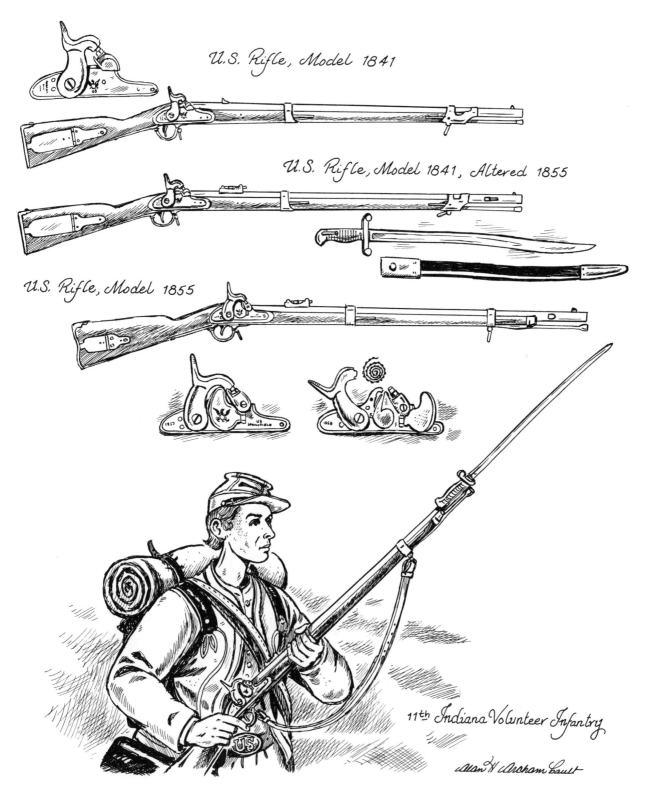

U.S. Rifle, Model 1841

U.S. Rifle, Model 1841, Altered 1855

U.S. Rifle, Model 1855

11th Indiana Volunteer Infantry

33

U.S. Rifle Muskets. Warfare was revolutionized during the mid 1800s by the invention of a hollow based conical bullet. Patented by a French Army officer, Captain Claude Minie, in America this bullet became known as the "Minie Ball." In 1855, the U.S. Army adopted the first weapon to use the new .58 caliber ammunition. Known as the Model 1855 rifle musket, the weapon also featured the Maynard tape primer. This system consisted of a roll of percussion primers which were fed on to the rifle musket's cone each time the hammer was cocked. At the beginning of the war, the Model 1861 rifle musket replaced the Model 1855 as the Army's standard rifle musket. Over 700,000 Model 1861s were produced and issued during the war making it the most widely used weapon of the Union infantryman. The Model 1861 was an improved version of the Model 1855, and was made without the unpopular tape system. Later in the war, a further refinement of the U.S. rifle musket resulted in the production of the Model 1863. This weapon had a redesigned hammer, barrel bands and ramrod.

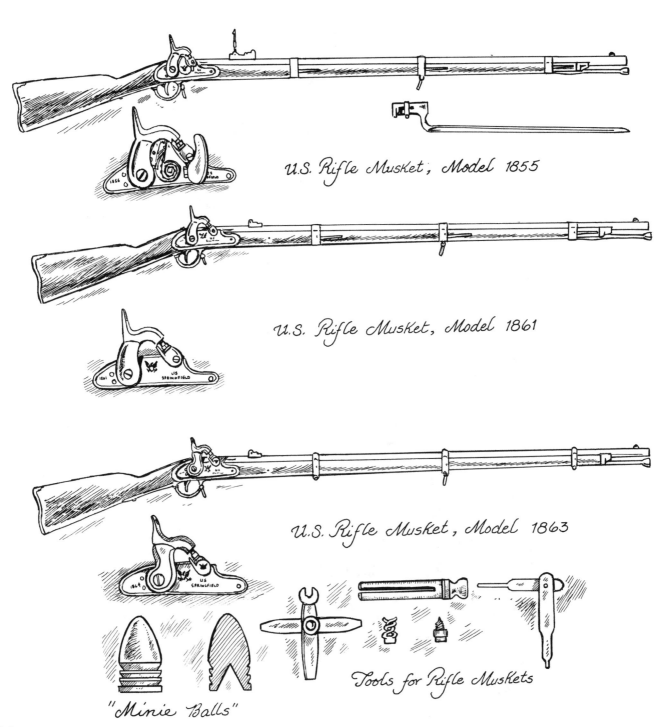

U.S. Rifle Musket, Model 1855

U.S. Rifle Musket, Model 1861

U.S. Rifle Musket, Model 1863

"Minie Balls"

Tools for Rifle Muskets

Loading a Rifle Musket. Although it took several distinct steps to load a rifled musket, a well trained infantryman could load and fire three aimed shots per minute. The basic steps in the process are illustrated here by a Union infantryman armed with a .58 caliber ,U.S. Model 1861 rifle musket, made at the Springfield Arsenal: 1. The soldier reaches into the cartridge box and removes a cartridge (note cross section of a cartridge and a .58 caliber "Minie Ball." 2. The paper cartridge is torn open with the soldier's teeth, exposing the black gunpowder. 3. The powder is poured into the muzzle of the rifle musket. 4. The bullet is placed in the muzzle.

5. The metal ramrod is taken from its position under the rifle barrel and rammed down the barrel, forcing the bullet and powder down to the bottom of the barrel. 6. A small copper percussion cap is taken from the cap pouch. 7. The hammer of the rifle musket is brought to the half cock position and the percussion cap is placed on the rifle's cone. The hammer may now be brought to full cock and the weapon is ready to fire. 8. When the soldier pulls the trigger the hammer falls on the cap which explodes and sends a flash through the cone into the barrel. This ignites the powder in the barrel which propels the bullet on its way towards its target.

British Weapons for Yankees. In the U.S. Government's efforts to arm the Northern infantrymen, agents were sent to Great Britain to obtain firearms. The weapons purchased from England were the best of all the foreign firearms issued to Federal troops. The Pattern 1851 rifle musket was issued to British soldiers during the Crimean War to replace their smoothbore muskets. It is believed that about 9,000 of these weapons were imported to the North in 1861. The Pattern 1853 rifle musket, known as the "Enfield" was the most popular of all the imported weapons of the war and second in use only to the U.S. Springfield. Over 500,000 were purchased by the U.S. Government between 1861-1863. The Pattern 1853 was made in .577 caliber which could fire the standard .58 caliber ammunition made for U.S. rifle muskets. The Pattern 1856 rifle, sometimes known as the sergeant's rifle, was a shorter version of the "Enfield" and was fitted with a saber bayonet.

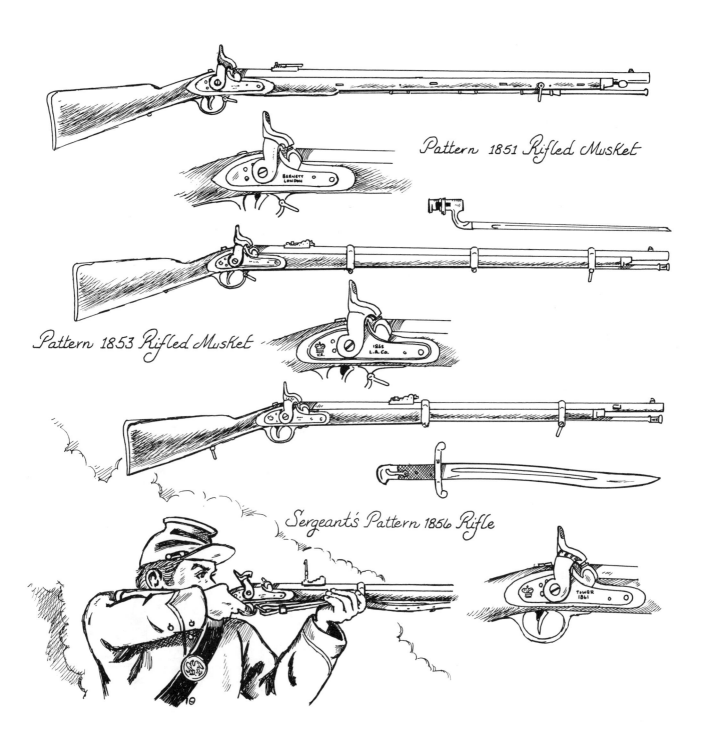

Pattern 1851 Rifled Musket

Pattern 1853 Rifled Musket

Sergeant's Pattern 1856 Rifle

Firearms from the Continent. By the summer of 1861, the United States was so desperate for weapons to arm the new volunteers that agents were sent to Europe to procure whatever arms were available. Surplus firearms from several countries, including France, Austria, and Prussia, were eventually purchased and shipped to the United States. Many of the weapons were obsolete, poorly designed firearms that were practically worthless. Other arms were found to be very serviceable. Regardless of their quality, these weapons helped to arm the Union forces until better weapons could be produced. All of the European muskets and rifles illustrated here were used by Union infantrymen at some time during the war. Eventually, most were replaced, when possible, by American manufactured rifle muskets.

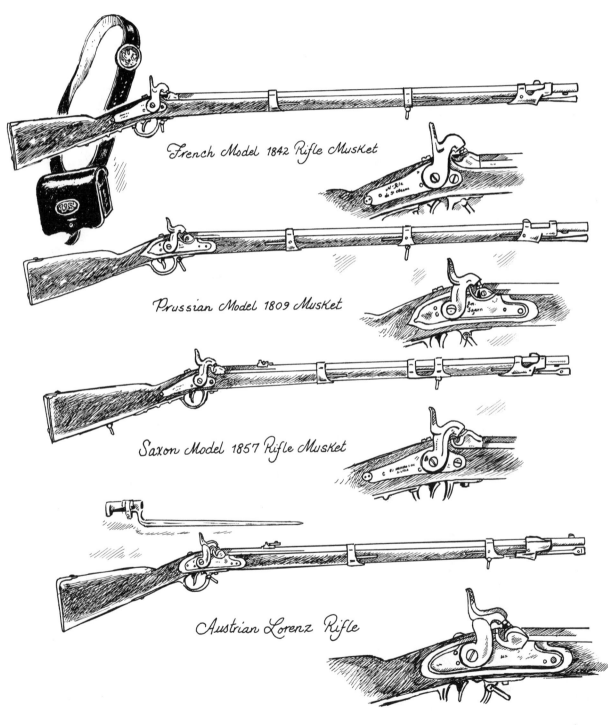

French Model 1842 Rifle Musket

Prussian Model 1809 Musket

Saxon Model 1857 Rifle Musket

Austrian Lorenz Rifle

Alan H. Archambault

Union Sharpshooters. No soldiers of the Union Army were more feared, or inflicted more casualties on the enemy, than the men of the two regiments of United States sharpshooters. The regiments were conceived and organized by Colonel Hiram Berdan who was a noted inventor and firearms enthusiast. Berdan staged shooting competitions in several Northern states to recruit suitable marksmen. In order to qualify, a recruit was obliged to place ten shots within a ten-inch circle at the distance of 200 yards. The sharpshooters were generally deployed as snipers and skirmishers where they could best use their skills against the enemy. Through most of their service Berdan's Sharpshooters wore distinctive dark green uniforms which had been the traditional dress of European marksmen. They were also issued fur-covered knapsacks and leather leggings. Generally, the sharpshooters used bugles, instead of drums, to convey commands on the battlefield. While Berdan's Sharpshooters served in the Eastern Theater with the Army of the Potomac, several other smaller units of marksmen were organized in the Northern states and saw action in campaigns in both the Western and Eastern Theaters.

Arms of the Sharpshooters. During their active service, the 1st and 2nd Regiments of United States sharpshooters used the weapons illustrated on this page. The sharpshooters were initially armed with Colt revolving rifles which were based on the design of the famous cap and ball revolver enlarged to .56 caliber. The revolving cylinder action of the Colt was prone to fouling and multiple discharges which could injure the rifleman's left hand. Although the sharpshooters were unhappy with the Colts, they used them until the spring of 1862 when they finally received the Sharps rifle. The durable and accurate Sharps was a .52 caliber breechloading single shot rifle which used combustible cartridges made of linen or nitrate treated paper. The Sharps issued to Berdan's Sharpshooters featured double set triggers which allowed the trigger pull of the weapon to be adjusted. For long range sniping the sharpshooters were equipped with heavy barreled target rifles. One of these weapons was the James target rifle which was a 14-pound, .45 caliber muzzleloader. It was used by Berdan's Sharpshooters during the siege of Yorktown, Virginia where it was accurate up to 500 yards.

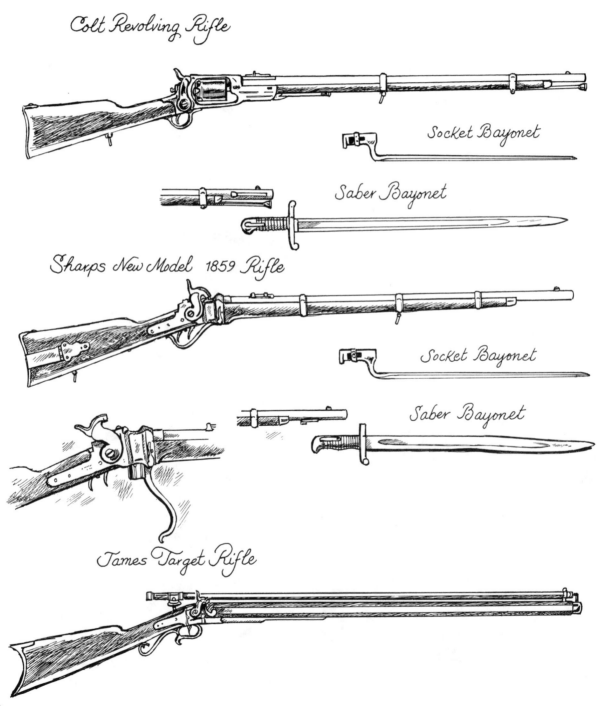

Colt Revolving Rifle

Socket Bayonet

Saber Bayonet

Sharps New Model 1859 Rifle

Socket Bayonet

Saber Bayonet

James Target Rifle

Repeating Firearms. Of all the firearms used by Union infantrymen during the war the Spencer and Henry rifles were the most technologically advanced. The Henry rifle was a .44 caliber, lever action, rifle that held fifteen rimfire copper-cased cartridges. Although the Army purchased only 1,731 Henry rifles, many soldiers privately purchased them for approximately $40.00 each. Over 10,000 Henry rifles were produced during the war with the majority being used by Union soldiers. In fact, the men of the 7th Illinois Volunteer Infantry purchased over 500 Henry rifles and were the only Union unit to be so armed. The firepower of the Henry was used to good advantage on several battlefields. The Spencer rifle became available in January 1863. It featured a tubular magazine which held seven .52 caliber metallic cased cartridges. The first units to be armed with the Spencer were independent companies of Ohio sharpshooters. The Spencer rifle also won fame in the hands of the mounted infantryman of Colonel John T. Wilder's "Lightning Brigade" which served with distinction in the Western Theater.

The Spencer Rifle

The Henry Rifle

Heroism. At the time of the Civil War, American society placed a great deal of importance on a man's bravery on the field of battle. In the days before our nation elevated athletes, musicians and movie stars to the status of celebrities, America's heroes were primarily soldiers and patriots. Since Union infantrymen went into battle with friends, neighbors, and family members by their side, they were aware that their manhood would be judged by their conduct under fire. Therefore, it is not surprising that great feats of courage were performed in battle. Many recorded acts of bravery involved the defense of the regiment's colors or the capture of the enemy's colors. In July 1862, Congress authorized the army Medal of Honor to recognize soldiers who performed feats of heroism "above and beyond the call of duty."

The National Colors. Contrary to popular mythology, the Stars and Stripes were seldom carried into battle during the American Revolution or the War of 1812. The national ensign did see some combat in the Mexican War, but it was during the Civil War that "Old Glory" saw its greatest use on the field of battle. Generally, each infantry regiment carried two flags into action: a regimental flag and a national color. The flags were made of silk and measured 6 feet by 6 1/2 feet so they could be easily seen on the battlefield. At the time of the war there was no set arrangement of the stars so a number of designs were used. The regimental designation was often painted on one of the stripes, as were battles in which the regiment participated. Two styles of national flag are depicted here as well as several examples of the finials which topped each flagpole.

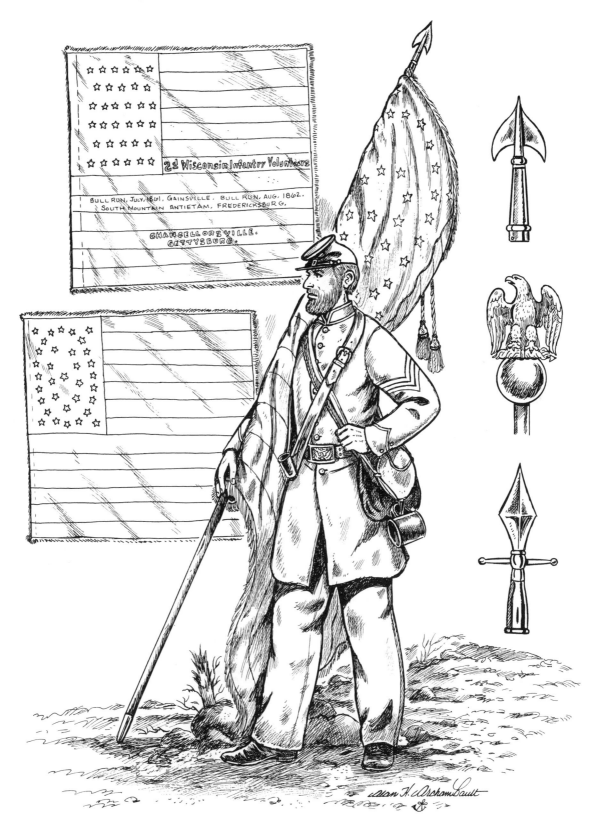

The Regimental Colors. Most Union infantry regiments were issued, or presented, with a regimental flag. Many of these flags followed the regulation Federal pattern which featured an American bald eagle, national shield, stars and a red scroll inscribed with the unit's designation. The flags were usually made of blue silk with gold fringe and blue and white tassels. However, a number of infantry units carried state issued flags into battle as well as many distinctive regimental flags which were emblazoned with unique designs or inscriptions. All these flags served the same purpose of promoting unit pride among the soldiers and serving as a rallying point on the battlefield. The men who carried the regiment's colors were most often sergeants and their courage served to inspire the soldiers in battle. Indeed, during many hard fought engagements, a unit that was retreating, or broken by the enemy, would rally behind a brave color bearer and continue the fight.

Infantry Officers. The men who led the "Boys in Blue" into battle were also responsible for organizing, training, and the administration of their men. Although a small percentage of the Union officer corps had formal military training, most were community leaders and other men of ability who were selected by state or federal officials to command various units. At the beginning of the conflict a number of officers were commissioned purely on the basis of political influence or social standing and some were even elected by the men of their respective units. However, as the war progressed, many of these officers were weeded out, as men of true ability proved themselves on active service. The average infantry company was commanded by a captain. He was assisted by a first lieutenant and a second lieutenant. Ten companies formed a regiment which was commanded by a colonel. The regimental staff usually consisted of a lieutenant colonel, a major, a regimental adjutant, quartermaster, a surgeon and a chaplain. This illustration depicts a typical regimental commander mounted on horseback and two company officers. The company commander is equipped for field service with a sack coat, slouch hat and boots. The lieutenant wears a short "shell" jacket, waistcoat, and a McDowell style forage cap. The company officers are armed with revolvers and Model 1850 foot officer's swords. The colonel carries a Model 1859 staff and field sword as a symbol of his rank.

Symbols of Command. Young company officers, like the one illustrated here, were important leaders on the battlefield. They directed the infantrymen in the line of battle and often their personal courage and dedication could make or break a unit's performance. A battlefield victory could often hinge on an officer's ability to lead and inspire his men. This second lieutenant wears a single breasted frock coat, crimson sash and forage cap. He is armed with a revolver and sword. Also depicted is an embroidered officer's hunting horn hat badge, a brass hunting horn cap insignia, a Model 1851 sword belt plate and shoulder strap insignia used to designate an officer's rank. For infantry officers these shoulder straps had a light blue cloth background and a gold border. **A.** Second Lieutenant **B.** First Lieutenant, one silver bar. **C.** Captain, two silver bars. **D.** Major, gold oak leaves. **E.** Lieutenant Colonel, silver oak leaves. **F.** Colonel, silver eagle. **G.** Brigadier General, one silver star. A major general was represented by two stars and a lieutenant general three stars.

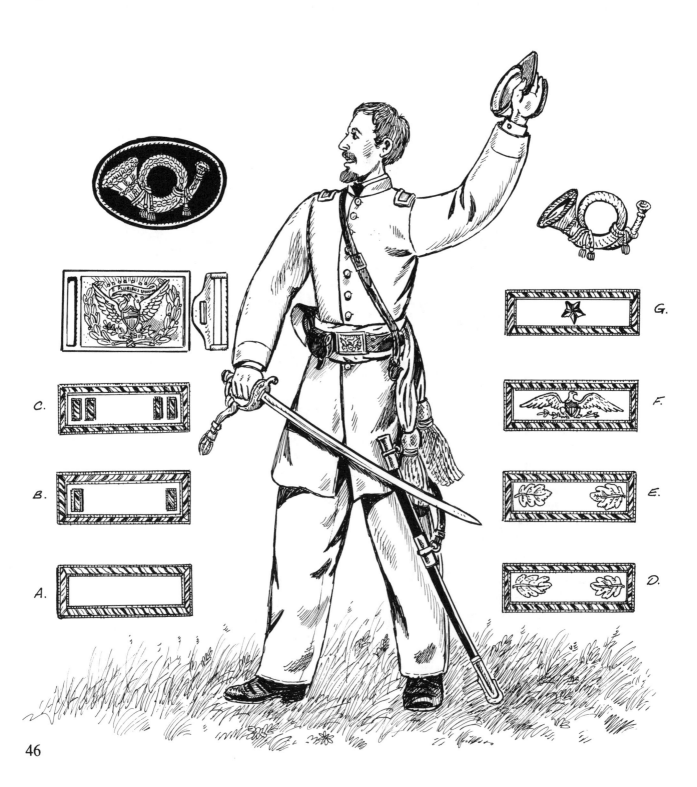

Noncommissioned Officers. Since the beginning of organized warfare, noncommissioned officers have been the backbone of every successful army. The sergeants and corporals of the Union infantry were responsible for the training of recruits and attended to the welfare of the men in camp and on campaign. Noncommissioned officers served as examples for the soldiers to emulate and acted as a liaison between the officers and enlisted soldiers. On the field of battle noncommissioned officers were positioned so that they could provide encouragement and direction to the men of the regiment. During the course of the war a number of noncommissioned officers who proved themselves in service were awarded commissions as officers.

Insignia of the Infantry Noncommissioned Officer. Rank was designated by chevrons worn on the sleeves of the noncommissioned officer's coat. The chevrons were made of light blue cloth and were worn with the points of the chevrons down. Sergeants were authorized to carry swords and a red sash as symbols of their rank. However, in the field few sergeants wore the extra finery. Soldiers who completed an enlistment in the Army were entitled to wear a service "half chevron" on their lower coat sleeves. Each chevron represented three years' service. For infantrymen, these service half chevrons were also made of light blue cloth. If an infantryman served an enlistment during wartime he was authorized to wear a light blue half chevron edged with red cloth.

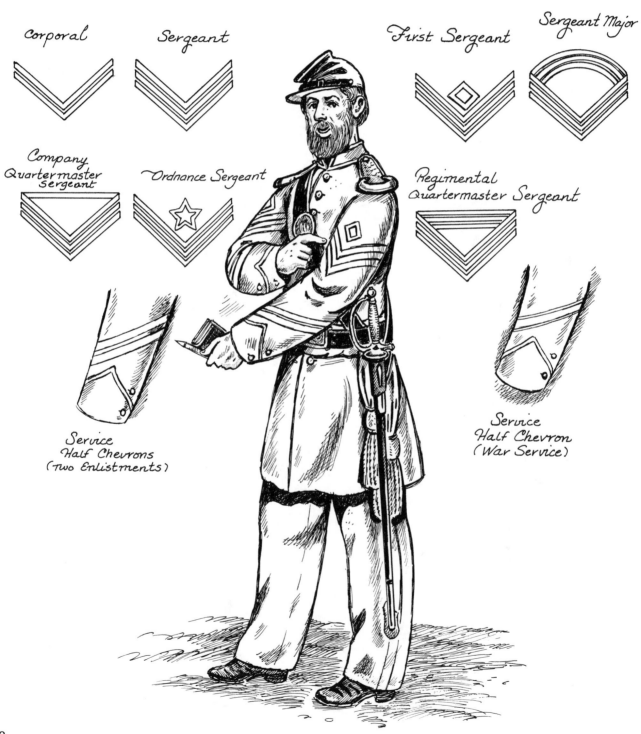

Corporal

Sergeant

First Sergeant

Sergeant Major

Company Quartermaster Sergeant

Ordnance Sergeant

Regimental Quartermaster Sergeant

Service Half Chevrons (Two Enlistments)

Service Half Chevron (War Service)

Patriots from Many Lands. During the 1860s, almost one third of the North's male population was foreign born. It has been estimated that one in every four Union soldiers was a first generation American patriot fighting for his adopted country. Germany was well represented with over 200,000 serving in the Union ranks. Some unit were predominantly German, with English as a second language. Many other nationalities served as well, including 50,000 Englishmen and a like number of Canadians. The 15th Wisconsin Infantry was composed primarily of Scandinavians including its commander, Hans Christian Heg, who was born in Norway. The 39th New York Infantry was known as the Garibaldi Guard, or Foreign Rifles. The unit included one company of Italians, one of French, three German, three Hungarian, one Spanish and one Swiss. The 79th New York State Militia was a prewar unit recruited from members of the Scottish community. Some soldiers of the 79th went off to war in full highland uniform, including kilts, but adopted standard Union uniforms for field service.

Sons of Erin. Of all the ethnic groups fighting for the Union the most celebrated were the Irish volunteers. It is estimated that more than 170,000 Irish-born soldiers served in the Union Army during the Civil War. In the decades prior to the war the great potato famine sent millions of Irish immigrants to the United States. However, in America, the Irish encountered hostility based on the anti-Catholic sentiments of many Americans. In spite of this prejudice, the Irish embraced their new country and when the war began they rallied to the cause of the Union. One of the first Irish units to see action was the 69th New York State Militia which fought at the First Battle of Bull Run in July 1861. Following the battle an Irish Brigade was formed which consisted of several Irish infantry regiments. The newly formed 69th New York State Volunteers joined the brigade and became its most famous regiment. The units of the Irish Brigade carried distinctive green regimental flags into battle and it is recorded that a general once exclaimed "where are my green flags?" The Irish Brigade became celebrated in song and story and the colorful conduct of the Irish volunteers, both on and off the battlefield, became legendary. The Irish Brigade saw action with the Army of the Potomac and won glory on many battlefields including Antietam, Fredericksburg and Gettysburg. This illustration depicts members of the Irish Brigade engaged in prayer prior to the Battle of Antietam in September 1862.

Zouaves. During the late 1850s, the romance of the French Algerian troops known as Zouaves, who won renown in the Crimean War, became popular in the United States. In 1859, Elmer E. Ellsworth, of Chicago, formed the U.S. Zouave Cadets who toured the country and popularized the uniforms and snappy drill of the Zouaves. When the nation went to war in 1861, dozens of Zouave inspired units were formed throughout the North. Some of the units were Zouaves in name only and their uniforms and drill were not based on true Zouave fashion. Other units, most notably the 5th New York Volunteer Infantry, better known as Duryee's Zouaves, were uniformed in full Zouave regalia, closely modeled on the style of the French colonial troops. After the initial "Zouave craze" of 1861, many of the units abandoned their Zouave status. However, a number of crack units like the 5th New York, 95th and 114th Pennsylvania continued to wear Zouave dress throughout their service in the war. This illustration depicts the 5th New York in action. This unit served with the Army of the Potomac in many hard fought battles. Their uniform featured a blue jacket and vest trimmed in red, full red pantaloons, and a red fez with gold tassel. A white turban was often worn around the base of the fez.

Corps Badges. The Union Army adopted corps badges in the spring of 1863 so that soldiers of the various corps and divisions could be distinguished. Major General Phil Kearny of the 3rd Division, III Corps actually had his soldiers affix red flannel diamonds to their caps in 1862, but it was not until Major General Joseph Hooker took command of the Army of the Potomac that corps badges began to be used on a larger scale. Originally, the badges were made of cloth and worn on the hat but eventually many soldiers procured embroidered or metal badges that were worn on the chest or hat. While the shape of the badge indicated the corps, the color indicated the division: 1st Division, red; 2nd Division, white; 3rd Division, blue; 4th Division, green; 5th Division, orange.

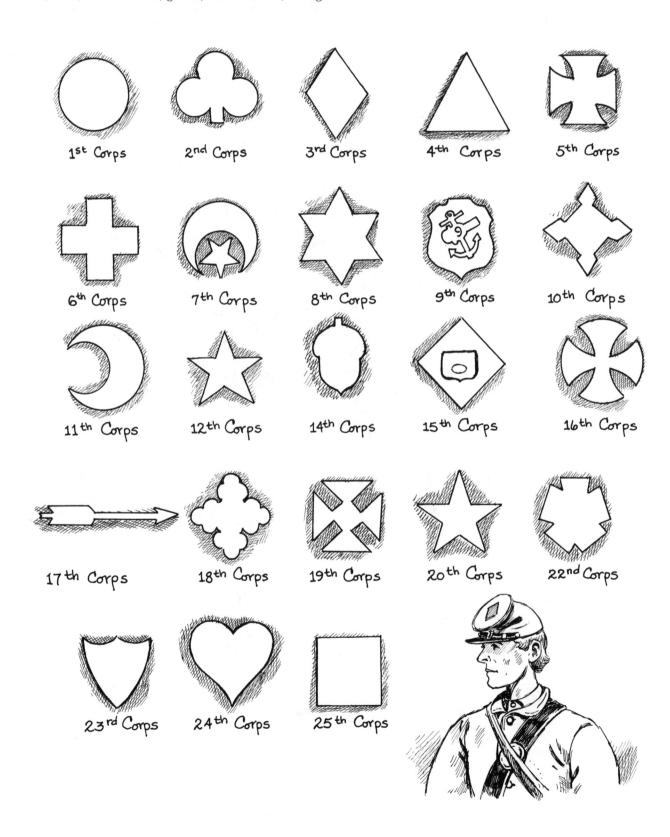

1st Corps   2nd Corps   3rd Corps   4th Corps   5th Corps

6th Corps   7th Corps   8th Corps   9th Corps   10th Corps

11th Corps   12th Corps   14th Corps   15th Corps   16th Corps

17th Corps   18th Corps   19th Corps   20th Corps   22nd Corps

23rd Corps   24th Corps   25th Corps

Discipline. From colonial times Americans have prided themselves on their independence and individualism. Therefore, it is not surprising that many Union infantrymen had a difficult time accepting the strict rules of military authority. A number of punishments were employed to teach the young Union soldiers the importance of military discipline and respect for authority. These punishments included carrying a heavy log around camp or marching with a knapsack of rocks. A soldier who showed disrespect to a superior was often "bucked and gagged." Placing a soldier in a wooden barrel or chaining them to a iron ball were other common punishments. More serious offenses such as cowardice or disloyalty could result in shaving the soldier's head and drumming him out of camp. The most serious offenses such as murder or desertion could be punishable by death.

Rations. One of the most important concerns to the Union infantryman was food. At the beginning of the war each Union soldier was authorized a daily ration of twenty ounces of fresh or salt beef, or twelve ounces of pork, a pound of flour, and a vegetable (usually beans). However, the rations issued to the Union foot soldier varied greatly during the course of the war. Although generally better fed than the Confederates, Northern soldiers often went hungry for lack of supplies. When in established camps, a company cook and staff were usually assigned the task of preparing meals for the soldiers. However, in the field, soldiers were issued the raw ingredients and were expected to cook it for themselves. The men formed small groups, called messes, and would pool their foodstuffs and assist each other in its preparation. A staple of the Union infantryman was a hard flour cracker called hardtack. This indigestible biscuit was often too hard to be eaten straight and was often soaked in their coffee or in stews. Meat most often came in the form of salted pork and coffee was the beverage of choice for most soldiers.

Recreation. Union soldiers were expected to create their own fun and diversions from the rigors of military life. Singing was such a popular pastime that the war years were called "the singing sixties." Union composers wrote over a thousand songs during the war, a number of which, like the "Battle Hymn of the Republic" and "When Johnny Comes Marching Home," are still sung today. Even though women were in short supply, Union soldiers often held "stag" dances among themselves. Reading and writing letters was also an important aspect of a soldier's life, as was reading newspapers and novels. Gambling, particularly cards, was a common vice which was frowned on by the officers and the folks at home. Baseball emerged from the war as America's favorite sport. Many soldiers learned the game in the army and took it home to their communities after their service. The soldiers depicted in this illustration are members of the 11th New York Volunteer Infantry, also known as the "First Fire Zouaves."

A "Civil" War. In spite of the fact that the soldiers of the North and South fought with such determination and ferocity on the battlefield, many of the men felt a certain amount of camaraderie with their foes. Both sides fought for what they believed to be right, but they learned to respect their battlefield adversaries as fighting men. Often, soldiers would exchange pleasantries, gossip, or even humorous taunts across the picket lines. When there were lulls in the fighting, adventurous soldiers were known to meet between the battle lines to exchange commodities. Northern soldiers would offer coffee, food and newspapers for Southern tobacco. The fraternization of the Blue and Gray during the war no doubt helped to ease the bitterness of the reconstruction period that followed the conflict.

Tenting Tonight. The average Union infantryman spent the majority of his military service "under canvas." A variety of tents were used during the war, most of them made from heavy white canvas. Officers generally lived in large wall tents which also served as headquarters tents. At the beginning of the war, most infantrymen used simple wedge tents which housed four to six soldiers. Sibley tents resembled Indian teepees and were invented by Henry Sibley in 1857. It incorporated a special stove whose stove pipe chimney ran up through a hole at the top of the tent. The Sibley, also known as a "bell" tent could sleep twelve or more men. By 1862, the army found that the transportation of tents and equipage was a logistical nightmare and began to issue small pieces of canvas to the infantrymen. Two soldiers would button their shelter halves together to form a small tent. When the first shelter tents were issued, the men nicknamed them "dog" tents because they were only large enough to house a dog. Soon the small shelter tents were the most widely used by the infantry when on campaign.

Winter Quarters. During the colder months of the year Civil War armies generally suspended major campaigning and went into winter quarters. It was during these winter months when armies would train and re-equip themselves for the coming spring campaigns. The soldiers were allowed to build cabins of logs and lumber. The cabins generally had fireplaces with chimneys made of sticks and mud or wood barrels. Often, canvas tents were used for roofs. The officer's quarters and regimental headquarters were often quite elaborate and comfortable. With the coming of spring the armies would usually abandon these rather comfortable log cities and resume their active service.

Taking Cover. As the war progressed, Union infantrymen, who once thought it cowardly to seek cover on the battlefield, learned that the protection provided by trees, rocks and fences could increase his ability to survive the battle. Early in the war, Union soldiers would often attack Confederate positions across open fields without using the natural terrain for cover. This resulted in terrible, needless, casualties. As the soldiers became veterans, they would try to advance on the enemy by moving forward in small groups taking cover whenever possible. When defending a position, Union soldiers would seek protection behind both natural defenses or would create "breastworks" from rocks, logs or whatever they could find that could stop, or turn, a bullet.

Digging In. As the frightful casualties took their toll on the infantrymen of both Union and Confederate armies, both sides began to construct and place more emphasis on fortifications. These defenses ranged from simple earthworks to elaborate trench systems. By the last campaigns of the war, the fortifications like those found at Petersburg, Virginia, foretold of the future battlefields of the First World War. Whenever possible, infantrymen built earthworks to protect themselves from enemy fire. Since average infantrymen were not issued shovels, bayonets, cups, and plates were often employed in building temporary field fortifications. During formal sieges, trench systems of wood and earth were constructed to provide protection. Wicker baskets known as "gabions" were also filled with earth and provided additional cover.

Health and Hygiene. Although the Civil War is noted for its battlefield casualties, far more soldiers died of disease than bullets. Approximately 224,580 Union soldiers died from sickness and disease. Early in the war much of the illness might have been prevented if soldiers had observed better sanitation and cleanliness. However, many volunteers understood little about cleanliness and germs and had to be taught the rudiments of good health and hygiene. It soon became apparent that the units that enforced personal hygiene had less illness in the ranks than units which had relaxed standards. By 1863, soldiers in the Union Army of the Potomac were required to wear their hair short, to bathe at least twice a week, and to change underwear once a week. These regulations, when enforced, helped to prevent the spread of disease and promoted good health.

The Veteran Reserve Corps. In April 1863, the United States Army established the Invalid Corps. The members of this corps were soldiers who were determined unfit for full field duty due to injury or illness but who could perform limited infantry duty. In March 1864, the corps changed its name to the more dignified, Veteran Reserve Corps. Eventually, twenty four regiments and 188 separate companies of veterans were organized to perform guard and garrison duty. Although the veterans were recruited to free more able bodied troops for field service, some members of the Veteran Reserve Corps saw action against Confederate troops, most notably at Fort Stevens, Virginia, in 1864. Enlisted members of the Veteran Reserve Corps were authorized sky blue jackets with dark blue trim while officers were to wear sky blue frock coats. The officers disliked the light colored coats and were eventually allowed to wear standard dark blue coats. Many of the enlisted men also adopted the dark blue sack coats of the regular infantry for service dress. This illustration depicts the Union Commander-in-Chief, Abraham Lincoln, saluting members of the Veteran Reserve Corps.

Black Infantrymen. In spite of the fact that black soldiers had fought with distinction in the American Revolution and the War of 1812, black men were not allowed to enlist in the Union Army at the beginning of the Civil War. Finally, after much debate, the Union Army was permitted to recruit black soldiers in late 1862. By the end of the war, 178,975 black Americans had served in the Union Army with the vast majority serving in infantry regiments. Although at first black units were often relegated to the backwaters of the war, they quickly gained the respect of their white comrades when they fought bravely in battle. By 1864, black soldiers had earned their place in the ranks of the Union Army and thirty eight regiments of black troops served in the decisive siege of Petersburg, Virginia. By the end of the war, no one could deny the important role that black soldiers played in the Northern victory and the preservation of the Union. This sketch represents a black infantryman talking to two recently freed children who look on him as a true hero. The regimental flag in the background belongs to the 12th Regiment U.S. Colored Troops.

Women of the Infantry. It should be remembered that a number of women also served with the Union infantry. At the beginning of the war, a number of Union infantry units followed the French Army's example of having "Vivandieres" attached to the regiment. These adventurous women provided assistance to the soldiers both on and off the battlefield, particularly nursing the sick and wounded of the unit. Although many vivandieres were sent home after the first battles, several women were documented to have served with the men through a number of hard-fought campaigns. Two of the better known women were Kady Brownell of the 1st and 5th Rhode Island Infantry and Marie Tebe of the 114th Pennsylvania Volunteer Infantry. Both were recognized for their courage and endurance. A number of other women were known to have dressed up as men and served in the ranks of the Union infantry. One such soldier was Jennie Hodgers of the 95th Illinois Infantry. Some of these women were discovered when they were wounded or ill, but others may have served as men without ever being detected. It has been estimated that several hundred women may have served in such a manner during the war. Depicted from left to right are Kady Brownell, Jennie Hodgers, and Marie Tebe.

Pets and Mascots. Many Union infantrymen adopted pets while on active duty. Individual pets included cats, raccoons, squirrels, badgers and other forms of wildlife. A number of infantry units adopted animals as mascots with dogs being the most popular. Jack was the canine mascot of the 102nd Pennsylvania Infantry and wore a silver studded collar presented by the soldiers. Major, a fearless mongrel attached to the 10th Maine Infantry was killed by a musket ball in battle, while the 11th Pennsylvania Infantry had Sallie, a female mutt, as its beloved mascot. The 12th Wisconsin had a tame bear as a pet and the 2nd Rhode Island was amused by the antics of Dick, a frisky pet lamb. The most famous Union mascot of the war was Old Abe, an American bald eagle carried by the 8th Wisconsin Infantry. Abe was tethered to a special perch and would flap his wirgs in the midst of battle. After the war, Abe lived in the state capital as a living memorial to the fighting men of Wisconsin. He died in 1881.

Brave Drummer Boys. Infantry soldiers lived to the beat of the drum so the youths who served as drummer boys have a special place in history. Although the average Union drummer boy was in his early teens some served as early as nine years old. Drummer boys were responsible for communicating commands to the troops so it was very important that they memorize the drum beats for each individual command. On campaign the drummers would often join in with fifers to provide music on the march and pick up the feet and spirits of the soldiers. Several drummer boys became heroes during the war because of their dedication and conduct in battle. The most celebrated drummer was young Johnny Clem who at the age of nine ran away to join the Army. He became known as "Johnny Shiloh" and later the "Drummer Boy of Chickamauga" because of his participation in those bloody battles. Although the bravery of the drummer boys was sometimes exaggerated by the sentimental public, there is no doubt that the young drummer boys provided examples of American courage and pluck.

Captured. During the war some 211,411 Union soldiers were captured by the Confederates. Most of these men were captured when their units were overrun by Rebel troops or when their commanders felt that further fighting was futile. Of these soldiers approximately 16,668 were paroled on the field with the agreement that they would not fight again until exchanged for Confederate prisoners. Unfortunately, 194,000 Union soldiers were confined in Southern prisons during the war where about 30,000 of them died. The conditions in Southern prisons were generally terrible with little food, bad water and unhealthy sanitation. Camp Sumter near Andersonville, Georgia became the most notorious of all Southern prisons and over 13,000 Union prisoners died there in less than a year. The intolerable conditions in Southern prisons was primarily caused by the shortage of supplies and by the inability to deal effectively with so many prisoners. It should be stated that living conditions for Confederate prisoners in Northern camps were not much better in spite of the North's ability to provide more food and supplies.

Wounded. It is estimated that about 275,175 Union soldiers were wounded in action during the war. The majority of these wounds, perhaps 94 percent, were caused by small arms, with a lesser number, about 5.5 per cent, caused by artillery fire. A very small number of wounds were inflicted with swords and bayonets. Those wounded soldiers who could walk would make their way to the rear of the fighting lines towards the regimental hospital. Generally, the regimental surgeon set up the hospital about two miles behind the battle lines. Those soldiers who needed assistance were often helped by other wounded comrades or by designated members of the regiment, such as bandsmen or other noncombatants. As the war progressed, the Union Army organized corps of stretcher-bearers and ambulances to assist with the wounded. In spite of primitive medical procedures and often inadequate treatment, almost six out of seven wounded soldiers survived their ordeal. Of course, those soldiers with serious wounds to the head or torso were most at risk to die. Soldiers with shattered arms or legs often faced amputation of the limb.

A Soldier's Death. The Union infantry suffered the greatest number of battlefield deaths during the war. Of the 110,100 Union soldiers killed or mortally wounded in battle the majority were foot soldiers. Small arms fire claimed the greatest number of lives and the Union infantryman was most at risk when attacking entrenched Confederate positions like those found at Fredericksburg and Cold Harbor, Virginia. Approximately 67,000 Union troops were killed outright, while another 43,012 were mortally wounded. Although poets and politicians romanticized a soldier's death in battle, the infantrymen knew that it was usually a painful and lonely end. The soft lead bullets fired by rifles and muskets caused ghastly wounds and smashed bones and muscles. It is a tribute to the courage and dedication of the infantrymen that they continued to charge into enemy fire knowing the risks and results of the carnage.

A Soldier's Resting Place. Following a battle members of the regiments engaged in the conflict would search for their killed and wounded. When a fallen comrade was found he was generally interred on the spot where he fell. His friends would dig a grave and carve his name, company and regiment into a board which was often pulled from a barn or a cracker or ammunition box. If possible, a prayer or hymn was recited over his grave. Later, it was usually arranged for the fallen soldiers to be re-interred in a military cemetery or sent home to his relatives for burial in a family plot. Many Union units had regimental funds to provide money to embalm the bodies and send slain comrades home for burial. Personal items found on the soldier, like letters and photographs were also generally returned to his family. Unfortunately, battlefield conditions did not always allow fallen comrades to be located and since most soldiers did not wear identification badges many soldiers were buried in unmarked graves, far from home and friends.

A Compassionate Victor. By the spring of 1865, the overwhelming armies of the Union had brought the beleaguered Confederate forces to their knees. In the Eastern Theater of the war, the defenses of Petersburg were finally breached by Union infantrymen and the once mighty Army of Northern Virginia began its march towards Appomattox Courthouse and defeat. On April 9, 1865, General Robert E. Lee surrendered his Confederate forces to Lieutenant General U.S. Grant, effectively ending the war in the East. Soon Confederate forces in other regions also surrendered to the victorious Union forces. However, the Union soldiers, particularly the humble infantrymen, often felt great compassion for his Southern counterpart. He realized how hard the Confederates had fought, and although happy that the war was ended, he took no joy in the defeat of so noble an enemy. Following Lee's surrender many Union soldiers gladly shared their rations with their hungry former enemies. This spirit of reconciliation among the fighting men was reflective of the honor and courage found in the ranks of both the Blue and Gray.

The Grand Review. In order to celebrate the end of the war and to commemorate the preservation of the Union, the War Department arranged a spectacular review of the Union armies in Washington, D.C. On May 23, 1865, the Army of the Potomac, some 80,000 strong, and led by Major General George G. Meade marched down Pennsylvania Avenue and passed in a proud review before President Andrew Johnson and other dignitaries and military leaders. On the following day, Major General William T. Sherman's 65,000 western veterans triumphantly marched in review to the adulation of the spectators. The Grand Review of the Armies was perhaps the most impressive military ceremony of the war if not in all American military history.

Mustering Out. In the months following the end of the war, many of the Union volunteer infantry units returned home. The arrival of each unit saw great emotion and celebration as loved ones and friends welcomed their returning heroes. Generally, fine banquets were held in honor of the veterans and the tattered battle flags were often presented to state officials with great and solemn reverence. Following the speeches, ceremonies and handshakes, the men were mustered out of Federal service. They were then free to hang up their suits of blue and resume their civilian occupations. The men could be proud that they had answered the call and preserved the Union for future generations of Americans. The Union had been restored!

Union Veterans. Although the war was over, most Union veterans did not want to end the associations and comradeship formed during the hardships of war. In 1866, the largest Union veteran's organization, the Grand Army of the Republic was formed in Illinois. Soon chapters, called posts, were formed throughout the North. The Grand Army of the Republic, often known as the GAR, not only served to host reunions but also lobbied for veteran's rights, pensions and patriotism. It was also involved in the establishment of Decoration Day, now known as Memorial Day, to remember those who had fallen to preserve the Union. Members of the GAR addressed each other as comrade and called their meetings encampments. Membership in the GAR grew as the veterans recognized its importance and by 1890 its membership peaked at 427,981. However, as the years passed, and the veterans departed this world, the membership eventually declined. The final encampment was held in 1949 with 6 of its 16 surviving members in attendance. Finally, in 1956, the last comrade of the GAR, Albert Woolson of Minnesota, once a Union drummer boy, passed into history.

The Legacy. In the years since the Union soldiers returned from the war, the legacy of their service has continued to live in the consciousness of many Americans. In Northern cities and towns statues of Union infantrymen often stand guard over an ever-changing landscape. A number of museums preserve memorabilia associated with the men who fought to save the Union and libraries contain thousands of books related to the war. Well-preserved battlefield parks also serve to remind Americans of their priceless heritage. The service and sacrifice of the Union infantryman also lives on in organizations comprised of descendants and in living history groups which portray Union infantry companies. The soldiers who preserved the Federal Union through the fire and storm of the Civil War deserve to be remembered by all Americans. However, perhaps their most fitting legacy is a strong and free United States. "One nation indivisible, with liberty and justice for all."

About the Author/Artist

Alan Archambault was born in Rhode Island and raised on a historic farm dating from the eighteenth century. Playing in the ancient fields and barns, he developed a keen interest in history and art at an early age. After service in the United States Army, Alan attended Rhode Island College and earned degrees in art and history. Through his artwork and writings, Alan strives to share his deep love for American history with others, particularly young people. Alan is married with two children and works in a studio in Lakewood, Washington.

Other Books in this Series

Thomas Publications is pleased to present this first volume of our ongoing sketchbook series on American history. The complete series will include the following titles.

Soldiers of the French and Indian War

Soldiers of the Revolution

Soldiers of the War of 1812

Soldiers of the Mexican-American War

Sketchbook of the Union Infantryman

Sketchbook of the Confederate Infantryman

Frontier Soldiers

Soldiers of the Spanish American War

The American Soldier of World War I

The American Soldier of World War II

Soldiers of the Korean War

Soldiers of the Vietnam War

American Folk Heroes

For Further Study

The following are a few other books available from Thomas Publications which will allow you to explore the era of the American Civil War in greater depth.

An Introduction to Civil War Small Arms by Earl J. Coates and Dean S. Thomas

Cannons: An Introduction to Civil War Artillery by Dean S. Thomas

Ready...Aim...Fire! Small Arms Ammunition in the Battle of Gettysburg by Dean S. Thomas

A Vast Sea of Misery: A History and Guide to Union and Confederate Field Hospitals at Gettysburg by Gregory A. Coco

The Civil War Infantryman by Gregory A. Coco

Civil War Commanders by Dean S. Thomas

Introduction to Civil War Photography by Ross J. Kelbaugh

Gettysburg Hour by Hour by Harry Roach

On the Bloodstained Field by Gregory A. Coco

Killed in Action by Gregory A. Coco

War Stories by Gregory A. Coco

An Introduction to Civil War Civilians by Juanita Leisch

A Strange and Blighted Land: Gettysburg, the Aftermath of Battle by Gregory A. Coco

THOMAS PUBLICATIONS publishes books about the American Colonial era, the Revolutionary War, the Civil War, and other important topics. For a complete list of titles, please write to:

THOMAS PUBLICATIONS
P.O. Box 3031
Gettysburg, PA 17325

Or visit our website at http://thomaspublications.com